EBENEZER FARNES

Ebenezer Farnes, 1843–1920

EBENEZER FARNES

AN AUTOBIOGRAPHY

Leanna Cressall Turley
David Roche Turley II
EDITORS

Anvil&
CROSS

Please direct questions and suggestions for future projects to

anvilandcross@gmail.com

PREFACE

The following is a transcription of the autobiography of Ebenezer Farnes. He wrote it sometime after February 4, 1910.

Social norms have changed since he wrote this work. These changes are evident in Farnes's use of antiquated racial language and his expression of cultural opinions. We have not removed them from the text to maintain accuracy in the transcription process. We have corrected spelling errors that do not seem to suggest accent or culture.

Farnes's autobiography has been cited in numerous publications because of his role in important historical events and his experience as a nineteenth-century member of The Church of Jesus Christ of Latter-day Saints.

Top row: Ebenezer Farnes, Matthew H. Farnes (brother)
Bottom row: Frances I. Farnes (sister), George I. Farnes (brother), Matilda S. Farnes (sister)

EBENEZER FARNES

Born February 4th, 1843, at Dagenham, Essex, England, about twelve miles east of London, England. Lived in Dagenham until about four years old, when my parents moved to London, where we lived until about nineteen years old. As a child I lived in several different places. My parents were very poor in my earliest recollections, my father having had his leg crushed and being too poor to pay for a good doctor, was an invalid for thirteen months and could not work, so my mother and seven children had to do the best they could.

When about six years old my two brothers took me out with them and came home by way of a canal where a barge loaded with all kinds of merchandise and coal for London consumption was hauled along the tow path by horses attached to a long rope. In following my brother along the side of the canal, I fell in the water and might have been drowned had not some people seen me and called to my brother to stop. However, a woman poked her umbrella out to me and saved me. I remember it was very cold and my clothes were frozen before we got home.

Up to eight years old, I had about six weeks in school, and after that none. In 1851 I took charge of a horse and trap for a commercial traveler named Call. My work was to clean the stable, bandage the horse's legs, harness him and sit in the trap while Mr. Call showed his goods to the customers.

At about eight years old I was a messenger boy for Waterloo Bess in London Wall, Bishopsgate Street, and worked here until eleven years old. After that I worked at printing as printers devil; butter shop, dry goods clerk, and several other occupations. My last job in England was in a dry goods store.

At about nineteen years old, in April, 1862, I emigrated for America, on the ship "Tapscott", with 852 passengers. This ship was a three-mast sailing vessel, old and worn out; an old tub not fit for merchandise, but good enough to carry "Mormons" on.

The ship was eight weeks and two days crossing the ocean. Before I left London, I had five young girls put in my charge to see that they got through all safe. Their names were: Jane Seamon, Eliza Pinnock, Emma Spencer, Fanny Penny and one more. When on board the ship I had five more put under my charge: Mrs. White and her four children.

The first day out of the harbor all the emigrants were sea sick and I was called on to help give out water and provisions, which I did until we landed in New York. The trip on the ocean was a red-letter day in my life. The first was rather rough and the second day rougher, and all the people were sea sick. After the fourth day out things on board ship went smooth and some of the people came on deck, others lay in their berths afraid they would die, and others afraid they wouldn't die. About the third week on the voyage there came a terrible storm which tore everything down that could be broken. So bad was the storm that the people had to stay in their beds for three days, the hatchway being closed most of the time, the water being one foot on the first and second decks, washing from one end of the ship to the other and side to side, as the ship tossed and rolled. The Captain said it was the worst storm he had ever seen and he had been a captain for twenty-five years. The ship sprung a leak and the pumps had to be kept going night and day until we reached New York. When the Captain was asked about the storm he said if he had known the condition of the ship, he would not have sailed on her, but consoled himself as he had a load of "Mormons" on board he would get through all right, as there had never been a ship lost that was carrying "Mormons". After the ship landed in New York, she was not considered fit to carry anything back but lumber, so they loaded her with that she got water-logged and was lost at sea. Taking the voyage all in all, it was quite an experience for us all, only two deaths, one child and a man who was sick when he came on board. The burial at sea is a sad thing. The body is sown in a canvas and a ball of iron placed at their feet so as to make the body sink feet first so the sharks cannot get it. A long plank is placed on the rail of the ship, part on the ship and part over the water, and the body is placed on the plank, feet to the water. After the burial ceremony the plank is lifted at one end and the body slides into the sea. You can see the body go slanting down for a long distance.

Besides having storms, we had calms which lasted from two to five days at a time. Sometimes we had drifted forty or fifty miles out of our course in all of one trip. We did not have favorable winds; all the winds were head winds, so we had to to tack. During the calm the emigrants had a good time playing on deck, climbing on the riggings, dancing and playing games. One game we played all the time; that was pumping water out of the vessel, about ten men at a time on the pump. One of them would sing all the time, making up the song as he pumped. Some of the words of the song were good and some ridiculous, but it helped break the monotony. I remember on one of the calm days the ship lay in the water rolling from side to side, and the porpoise, a fish from four to six feet in length and as fat as a pig, was playing about the ship and the water like a sheet of glass. Myself and some of the other young men started to climb the rigging. We chose the middle mast because it was the highest. We had climbed about half way up and the sailors thought they would have some fun by catching us up in the riggings and tying us up to the mast. They caught one boy at the top of the mast having a good time, and a boy named Kent was waiting for me to come down so he could climb to the top. The sailors thought to catch me and tie me. Now up in the rigging there is not standing room for two so they stayed at the third landing from the top and let the Kent boy go down, so they could catch me and tie me. About sixteen feet from the top is a guy rope that runs down to the side of the ship deck to hold the mast steady. Instead of coming down the mast to where the sailors were, I swung on to the guy rope and slid down to the deck. The rope had been lately tarred and was not dry, and I was skinned and covered with tar from my ankles to my thighs. The sailors said I would have full run of the ship from that time on, and so I was quite a favorite among them.

Things went along in about the same old style, head winds and calms, and we got short of fresh water and were put on half rations, but a last, after eight weeks and three days on the ship, we landed in New York, stayed there two days and got on board the train. The train service was pretty good until we got to Niagara Falls. Yes, the Falls are the grandest sight I have seen yet, water and mist, and the swift current below the falls is a sight beyond my description. We crossed the Niagara about half a mile below the falls on the new suspension bridge. After crossing the bridge we changed cars, and such cars, common cattle cars, with all the filth left from the last load of cattle, all wet and stinking. We traveled very slow in Canada on account of it being a new road. The engine would have to stop on some of the upgrades and get up steam and then go on again for a few miles. So slow was the train that the people could get out and walk the grade and some of the young folks would get around the gars and push to give them a start.

Just as we got to the line between Canada and the United States, some bush rangers tried to wreck our train. They loaded a trolly car with rails and as we came down a steep grade, they started the trolly car down the grade so as to meet us at the bottom. Our engine struck the trolly car and three cars went over the fragments of the trolly car. After three hours work, we started on again and the next change of cars was better. Eventually we got to Chicago, where I got left. We did not expect our train to leave until 1:00 p.m. It was then about 11:40 a.m. A brother named Price asked me to go and get him some eggs and bread and gave me twenty-five cents to pay for them with. I started for them and crossed the draw-bridge; that is a bridge that opens in the center so that small vessels can pass up or down the stream. I got twelve eggs and two loaves of bread and was on my road back to the train and, to my horror, the drawbridge was opened and I heard the train whistle, all aboard. After a few minutes the bridge closed and I ran as fast as I could. I got to the station just in time to see the last end of the cars and a boy saw me and pointing his finger at me said: "Ma, Ma, there's a Mormon left behind". To describe my feelings would be impossible, for my last hope had flown. There was I in my shirt sleeves, canvas hat, canvas pants and canvas shoes that a sailor made for me after my escape in the rigging; no money or coat, simply left alone in Chicago.

After collecting myself together I went to the ticket of-fice to see how I was to go on my way to the valley. The ticket agent could not help me any, and, as I stood pondering and feeling if not looking picture of despair, I heard a sweet voice gently say: "Was you a traveler on the special emigrant train?" I looked in the direction of the voice and saw the prettiest German girl it had been my lot to see, sitting behind a fruit stand. She asked me if the ticket agent could not help me and I told her no, so she advised me to go to the general office and state my case. She directed me and I went and state my con-dition and was told to come back in an hour. I went back in that time and received a pass on the Chicago Burlington and Quincy Railroad and was told to take the 6:00 p.m. freight train. Feeling all O.K. I sauntered back to my little German girlfriend and told her about my good luck. She looked at my my pass and said it was as good on any train at any time, and advised me not to take the 6:00 p.m. train as that only traveled 15 miles an hour, and the emigrant train went twenty miles an hour, and that I would never catch my train, but if I waited until 10:00 p.m. the Postal Express started then and would pass the emigrant train at 8:00 a.m. next morning. I had confidence in what she told me and waited until 10:00 p.m. During the interval I walked about Chicago, visited the barracks, and principal street and the shore of the lake, and had quite a good time. I saw one man killed in a runaway, saw some rebel prisoners (it was during the war which had just broken out and these were hot times generally.)

After seeing Chicago I got on board the express train and started. The only person I saw was an old lady who thought I was a train hand and asked me something about the train. After riding four hundred miles at forty miles an hour, the train stopped and I saw another train on a side track, just as my German girl told me I would. It did not take me long to get off the express and when the people on the train saw me they set up a yell that would almost wake a drunken man. Oh such hand shaking. They were so glad to see me that they all wanted to shake hands with me at once. After a little while our train started and got to St. Joe, Missouri. There we took a boat for Florence, the outfitting place for our start on the plains by ox team. The steam boat that carried us up the Missouri River was a day making the trip. It was very hot on the trip, three people dying from heat and drinking ice water. The three dead people were buried on the bank of the river. At last we got to Florence, where the emigrants pitched their tents and started to learn to rough it. Florence is a few miles north of Omaha and had some of the worst storms I have seen. One storm in particular, the water came down in sheets. It rained so hard that it hurt the skin wherever it struck, and lightning killed three persons and a great many more were injured.

After lying about for two days I got a job waiting on table at the hotel and fared quite well, having plenty to eat and not much to do. After about two weeks in the hotel, W. S. Godbe, a druggist of Salt Lake City, who was fitting out a freight train to cross the plains, asked me if I would come and cook for his men who were fitting up the wagons. So I told him yes. I started to cook for him and was to cook across the plains. After about three weeks of that work the ox team was ready. The Captain, Ben Hampton, came to me and said: "Well cook, I shall have to make a teamster of you until I can get a teamster". He handed me a long whip about fourteen feet long and showed me five yoke of cattle. He said: "The wheelers are good and the leaders are broke to work, the other three yoke are wild, and we will help you to yoke them up for a few days".

You can imagine my surprise. I had not even seen an oxen yoked and did not know how to drive them. Well, the leader of the wagon train started the first team, and the rest of us piloted our cattle behind and we traveled about ten miles a day the first day on our journey of one thousand miles across the American Desert.

The next day all were busy cooking breakfast and yok-ing cattle. Most of the boys did not know their cattle, myself among the rest. After some hours hard work we got started and all went well until one leading team got stuck in a slew and the next team tried to cross above and got stuck also. There were five teams all stuck at one time. Then our Captain, Ben Hampton, put twelve yoke of oxen on one wagon and tried to pull it out, but the chain breaking and at last we had to unload the wagons and pull them out empty. That day we did not travel far. The next day we got started earlier in the day and so traveled about fifteen miles, as we got used to hitching up our cattle. We drove long distances until the first crossing of the Platte River was reached; that took us two days. After that we drove fifteen to twenty-three miles per day.

The Platte River bottom is a very level country with beautiful green grass as far as the eye can see. We made good time until reaching the sand hill. There we traveled slowly as we had to put two teams on one wagon to cross. The cattle stood it fine until we got to the hilly country, and then they got foot sore and lame. We began to get in the Buffalo country as in traveling along we could see small bands of buffalo almost any time. On one occasion we had to stop five hours in order to let a herd of buffalo pass across our path, as it was not safe to get close to them, for they will not turn out of the way of their course, but will follow the leader through hills, rivers, freight trains, or anything else. The black hill country was well supplied with large game, viz; deer, antelope, sheep, buffalo, bears, porcupines, and wolves, so a man that is good with a gun need not want for fresh meat. There were also plenty of fish in the streams and wild fowl along the banks.

We made pretty good time on the plains, but it became

monotonous day after day, the same old thing; get up in the morning at 4:00 o'clock, make a fire, cook breakfast, eat and get ready to start at 6:00 or 7:00 a.m. It was hard on me as I had a very bad leg through a kick one of the boys gave me because I beat him in a wrestling match. My leg got so bad that my shin bone was bare for four or five inches and made me very lame, but I got along as well as I could riding in the wagon sometimes on good roads, until we reached Green River. The river was high that year and it was very dangerous to cross it. However, the Captain found a gravel bar so that we could cross the stream. We started to cross when the third team got stalled in the river and my leg hurt me so much standing in the water up to my waist that I started to pass the team that was stuck. The captain saw me and came dashing up to me and commanded me to stop for if I had gone twenty feet further across the stream my team, wagon and myself would have gone down the river and perhaps been lost, as the bar in the river was narrow and there was not room for two teams to pass each other. I had to stand in the ice cold water for more than an hour. At first my leg hurt me, then got numb, at last it seemed no use to me. I had to drag it along like a piece of lead, but at last we got across the river and camped. After turning our cattle out to feed I got back to the river and took my boot off and the sight of my poor leg made me feel sick. The flesh of my leg around the sore place looked all white like a piece of boiled tripe. In pouring water on it the water ran out of a hole in my heel. I wrapped up my leg and thought perhaps I could get to Utah and then have it taken off. Pleasant thoughts for a young man all alone in the desert, but from that day forth the sore did not pain me so much and day by day the wound got smaller and smaller, so when we got to Salt Lake City the wound was more than half closed and soon got well.

After crossing Green River things went O.K., some days climbing steep hills, going down deep canyons, and there was very little level ground until we got to the valley. We camped on the Eighth Ward square the first night and unloaded our freight next day.

On the third day we were paid off and my pay for the journey was $35.00. I bought an ax and the next day started on foot for Grantsville, forty miles to the West, taking all y belongings on my back. I arrived at Grantsville the same evening, very tired and hungry. My sister Mary and her husband were very glad to see me and made me welcome.

At Grantsville I soon got work, sometimes on a threshing machine, other times digging potatoes, shucking corn, turning the fan mill, etc. In those days the threshing machine did not separate all the wheat from the chaff as they do now, and about one-third of the wheat had to go through a fan mill to get the chaff out. A day's work was a bushel of wheat worth two dollars, or other things in proportion; molasses two dollars a gallon, potatoes seventy-five cents per bushel, corn one dollar and fifty cents per bushel, and meats, if you could get them, were twelve cents per pound. There was no money here at the time so wheat was the trading standard at two dollars per bushel. After a week my brothers M. H. Farnes and George I. Farnes, came down from Cache Valley to see me, and it was a joyful meeting. We talked about what would be the best way to bring our mother and father and sisters out to the valley, and we concluded to go to Salt Lake City and see what we could do about it.

Hearing that the Church blacksmith shop was in need of charcoal, we saw the authorities and made a contract to furnish them with one thousand bushels of charcoal and they would bring them from Florence, Nebraska, and from there the Church would bring them on to Utah through the perpetual emigration fund, and they were to pay the balance when they could.

We started back to make arrangements to burn the charcoal, but neither M. H. or myself had ever seen a charcoal pot burn, so we had to depend on our brother George. After a few weeks we got started to the mountains to chop our cedar for the coal. We selected a place about eight miles west of Grantsville and put up a brush shack covering the top and sides with cedar limbs. We built a chimney in one corner so that we could have a fire in it and not burn the house. Under the circumstances it was pretty good. Of course the wind would blow through and the snow would come in at times and our bedding would get wet, but we were contented and set to work with a will. We got a lot of wood cut and hauled and the bark peeled off and we had enough wood to make thirteen hundred bushels of coal and we were very happy. George Farnes superintended putting up the pit. We built a wooden chimney and laid some small pieces at the bottom so that when the pit was completed we could drop some fire down the chimney and start the coal burning. We got our coal pit finished with draft holes along the bottom, covered the wood with cedar bark, and then covered it all over with soil about five inches deep. We set fire to it and it caught splendidly. My two brothers and Samuel House watched the fore part of the night and reported everything doing fine. It was burning fine, I must say, for there was a stream of fire going out the chimney about twenty feet high. The boys went to bed and it was my watch until morning. After watching it for some time I thought there was too much blaze and tried stopping the draft holes, but it did no good. The blaze got bigger and bigger, so I climbed to the top so that I could see into the pit, and, my gracious! there was a hole burnt in the middle of the pit large enough to turn a yoke of cattle and a wagon in it. I called the boys and told them the condition of things and to say that they were excited is putting it mildly. Something must be done and that quickly too. The ground was frozen hard and dirt was out of the question. We threw four cords of wood into the fire and it burned as quickly as it went in. We put snow on it and the straw from our beds, anything that we could pack, and at last we got the worst of the fire under control. By beating the top and packing it down we got it to smouldering and about ten days afterward we uncovered our coals and got 160 bushels of coal in the place of 1200 bushels. We were the most discouraged boys you ever saw. We had cut all the wood there was near, the winter most gone, our provisions gone, and we had for our winters work, four of us, 160 bushels of charcoal. The four were, G. I. Farnes, M. H. Farnes, Samuel House and E. Farnes. Rather discouraged but not disheartened, we started to haul what we had to the city. M. H. Farnes thought it best for two of us to go with the first load so on Sunday morning we went up the canyon and cut a load of wood. He and I went up early next morning to get it. We got it loaded and got about one-half a mile down the canyon when we broke a wheel. We had to go home for another wheel and that broke down also. Wednesday morning we borrowed the hind part of a wagon and came down O.K.

Samuel House, thinking we could catch him, started for the city with the coal early in the morning. Just as I was starting from Grantsville with the load of wood here comes Samuel back with the cattle and no wagon. His axel had broken in the middle of a level road about six miles from home. You can see we were up against it. We rented another wagon and put our charcoal in that and I started to Salt Lake City alone and got there the next day. On inquiry I found that the best method of burning charcoal was in small pits so we put up some small pits and were successful, and by spring had finished our contract.

Some little incidents of our trials during the winter; In the first place we only had one yoke of cattle and when we wanted to use them we could seldom find them, so after looking for them for two or three days we would hire a yoke of cattle from the range, work them for a few hours, and then turn them out again. One time we had taken a yoke of cattle from the range to haul some cedars to our camp and they would not pull the load down the hill, so M. H. started for camp for something to make them pull. When he got to camp there was a man asking if we had seen such a yoke of cattle, so we directed him the opposite direction, and after he had done the cattle pulled the load down with ease. We turned them loose again and thanked our lucky stars that they had refused to pull, for if they had come down the first time we would have met the man and then we would have had trouble on our hands.

Once we went three days with nothing to eat except dry corn and that did not satisfy our craving for food, so I started for the settlement on a run and had gotten about half way when I met Samuel House with about twenty pounds of flour, and returned to camp. We got our supper and retired. When we ran short of food M. H. would go to the settlement and tinker, as he was a tinner by trade, and he would earn considerable toward our grub. Taken all together it was a hard proposition in the dead of winter, up in the mountains, and our clothes wet all the time as we were working in snow up to our waists most of the time. With wolves and coyotes howling all the time and very little to eat, we accomplished our purpose and were very thankful. I wrote a letter to the folks in England telling them what we had done for them, and to be ready to start for the valley. We could not get twenty-five cents to pay the postage in all Grantsville, so I put up one dozen eggs and started on foot for Salt Lake City to sell them, and I had a hard time to get cash for them. At last one man gave me twenty-five cents, Salt Lake currency, and the post master refused it because it was not United States currency. I took it back and the man gave me two ten-cent pieces and one three-cent piece and the post master refused that because it was one cent short, as it cost twenty-four cents to post a letter to England. I went back again and the man gave me back my eggs very indignantly. There must have been something in my disappointed look that softened the man's heart, for he spoke to

15

me kindly and I told him I had walked forty miles that day to get a stamp for my letter, and its purpose. He looked over his currency and found a twenty-five cent postal currency, gave it to me and I went back the third time and posted my letter. Not having any relations in town I started on my way back to Grantsville, walked all night and got home at 7:00 o'clock the next morning, after walking eighty miles in twenty-four hours to post a letter.

After staying in Grantsville for short time I went to the city and got work from Archibald Hill in the Fifth Ward. My work was digging a ditch around a small farm. After I had done all the work he had for me, he recommended me to the Tithing Office to drive a team. After a short time I was asked to ride an express to Tooele settlement, a distance of thirty-five miles. I made the trip there in less than four hours. Major Harris was dying so I was sent to tell his son, Alex Harris, it being my first ride on horseback for any distance it made me very sore from heel around to the other heel.

In the fall of '63 I was asked at a minute's notice if I would take a pony team and go back on the plains alone and meet all the companies and ask them if they would need any tents and transact other business. I told them I was ready to start that day, so they started me off without any provisions or cook. I took twelve tents, some oats for the horses, some flour and some bacon. I tried to buy some bread but could not get it. I traveled about forty miles a day, rather lonesome, but then I should see my father, mother, and my sisters on the way. I met several of the companies of the saints and delivered my instructions to them and left tents for those that wanted tents and got provisions for myself.

One evening I camped at the Pacific Spring. At the South pass at this place there are two springs not forty yards apart, one of them running into the Pacific Ocean and the other empties into the Atlantic Ocean. It is the divide and a cold place at any time. The night I camped there it was colder than usual and I took a cold chill. There I lay in my wagon, shaking and rattling the wagon so bad that I wonder that there was a bolt left in it. The wind blew and the wild animals howled. My horses were restless and I was sick and lonesome indeed. The next morning was welcome to me so I started on again having had no supper or breakfast. In traveling along the side of the road I saw a parcel wrapped in a newspaper and on picking it up, to my surprise, I found a large loaf of warm bread. Who had left it there? I looked for the track of a horse or wagon but could not see the first sign of any. The ground was soft and the small grass and weeds had covered the track of the last team that had gone over the road, but whoever left it there I was very thankful for them for it an after traveling about twenty miles that day I met a man named Rhodes from Weber and he was very good to me. He thought we were on the wrong road as there had been considerable rain and the road had grown green with grass, and it looked as if it had not been traveled since the year before. After leaving the Big Sandy River, about ten miles east, my team became restless and wanted to run.

I was surprised and thought perhaps some of the harnesses were loose. In looking behind me I saw a band of Indians all in their war paint. They rode up on each side of my team and made signs for me to stop, which I did as soon as I could get control of my team, at which time one of the Indians spoke to me in his language, which of course I could not understand, then he spoke in fair English and asked me what was in my wagon and I told him. He asked me who sent me and I told him Brigham Young, and he opened my shirt to see if I had garments on. I had not, so he said: "You chump, you lie". After considerable talk I persuaded them that I had told the truth and after giving them about one third of the provisions I had, they turned back and were soon out of sight.

In 1863 the Indians were on the war path and killed many private companies crossing the plains, but they did not molest the Latter-day Saints, and I found afterwards that they eighty Indians who stopped me were Pawnee Indians and were after a band of Sioux Indians to fight them.

I traveled rather nervously afterward, knowing that the Indian were bad and perhaps then next time would not let me off so easily, but I did not meet any more. The next day I expected to meet my folks, but about noon I met two men on horseback. I asked them how far Captain McArthur's train was behind, and they told me about three miles. I asked if a family named Farnes was in the train, to which they replied: "Yes, your father died yesterday", and rode on. The blunt way in which he told me was almost more than I could stand. The contrast between feelings before and after he answered me is too great to imagine. The joy I hoped to experience upon meeting my father and mother and loved ones soon was dispelled by the knowledge that my father had died the night I camped at the South Pass. It broke me down. I stopped my my team and could go no further, as I felt my heart would break at meeting the train. I lay beside the road weeping tears from the heart if there is such a thing. After a while the train came in sight and they passed me, but I could not muster courage enough to meet my mother. After a time I drew myself together, Knowing they would camp soon, I hitched up my team and turned back and overtook the company, just as they were making camp. I found the wagon they were in and after a while went there and found my mother in a burning fever; the mountain fever, we call it Typhoid fever. My mother did not know me. She thought I was M. H. and called me her Matthew. My sister Matilda was just getting over the fever while the others, Jane, John S. Farnes and Mary Ann French, were worn out with sickness and the death of father. Father had walked from early morning until 11:00 p.m. and while putting up a tent for the girls, fell down three times and was dead in less than an hour. He died at 12:00 p.m. and was buried at daylight with the dead sweat all over his body, and all this hurry because Captain Andrew McArthur of St. George, wanted to make a record of making the best time and bringing his cattle in the best shape across the plains.

Well, he did it, but how many human beings were caused to suffer for his record? After staying at the camp until the ox teams were ready to continue the journey, I bid goodbye to my mother and sisters, never expecting to see them again, especially my mother. It was hard for me to turn my back on them and go three hundred miles east. A young man volunteered to go back with me and show me the way and where my father was buried. My intentions were to dig up the grave and see if he was dead when they buried him, as one of the men who helped to put him away told me he did not think father was dead, as his shoulders were warm with sweat.

The next day we saw one of the sights of the desert. Near the crossing of the Sweet Water River there had been a larger number of cattle die at one time, and they were lying in the center of the road and there were seventy-five or eighty large prairie wolves eating the carcasses, and about one hundred coyotes waiting until the wolves were satisfied.

These wolves were large ones and could easily have eaten my team and both of us in less than an hour. I did not feel afraid of them as they had plenty to eat, they will only attack a man when they are hungry or wounded. Well, it was a sight to see with their long hair and bush tails shining in the sun, with their red mouths open and their teeth snarling at us as we passed them, some of them not more than twenty-five feet from our team. It was quite a relief when we got passed them and out of sight. Few men have seen such a large number of grey wolves at one time.

That evening we got to the place where father was buried. The grave was all that anyone could ask for under the circumstances. After a few hours rest we journeyed east and soon met another emigrant train, where we stayed all night, left some tents, delivered our message and started on again. At length we met the last company with Captain White, on the Platte River, and we set our faces to the West, traveled with that company a few days and then left to catch up with the next company ahead, which we did, and stayed two days.

This company was under Captain Hyde, in which a woman committed suicide, as hereafter related. After being with this company an hour, a sister came up to me and asked to go to a poor Welch woman and try to get her to take something to eat, as she had not been out of the wagon for two days. She and her husband had been quarreling two days before and she was sulky. I went to the wagon and spoke to the woman, but received no answer. I looked closer and could see part of her legs, her body being covered. I put my hand on her and asked her to get up as there was a brother from Salt Lake City who wanted to talk with her, and again received no answer. I told her if she did not get out I would pull her out by the feet. No answer came, so I started to pull her by the ankle and found she was dead. it did not take me long to drag the bed clothes from her and then found that she had smothered to death. her face was in the bottom of the wagon box and the rest of her body about two feet and a half higher. Her face and neck were black and mortifying. She evidently had put her head at the bottom and pulled the clothes over her body and the teamster not knowing, had thrown his bed clothes on top of her and had been sitting on her head for two days.

We made an investigation to see if there had been any foul play, but could not find anyone to blame but herself, so we dug a grave, wrapped the body in the bed clothes she died in, and put her in the hole, which was deep and the men who buried her had to drop the body the last foot or so and the sound of the thump as the body struck the ground is still sounding in my ears. When we threw the soil on the corps I had to go away as I could not stand the sound. I thought of my poor father and his burial in a similar manner.

Well, we traveled with that company that day and then went ahead again, traveling about thirty miles when we came to the last crossing of the Sweet Water, where we found a small company of United States Soldiers camped. As we drew up the soldiers were lined up on each side of the road and appeared to be drilling, so we turned out to go around them.

They threw out a flank and headed me off, so I went to go around the other way, but they surrounded me and took me a prisoner of war, it being during the rebellion between the North and South. These one hundred and fifty soldiers were sent back on the plains to search the Saints' companies crossing the plains to see if they had any gun powder, and if so to confiscate it.

There was a company of "Mormon" boys following up on horseback, and as all the Saints had been notified of the soldiers being on the road, they had disposed of all their gunpowder and these boys by a roundabout way brought the powder to Salt Lake City, Utah. These boys did not travel by the road, but kept in the background so that when the soldiers searched the wagons they did not find any powder. Thinking that I must have been the means of their not getting any powder, they stopped my team as I was coming back home, while they searched the last companies. When the commander told me they would have to hold me a prisoner I told him all right, so long as he fed me and my team and he assured me that I should fare just the same as the rest of the company, and not to feel myself under any restraint and consider myself his guest until his return from searching the last two trains. Soon after the captain left the camp with one hundred of his men, leaving thirteen to guard me, one of the soldiers took the hay from my horses and swore at me for feeding the hay to my horses as there was not enough for their own. So, I had to turn my teams out to shift for themselves. There not being any feed nearby, my horses crossed the river. The next morning as I was crossing the river to feed my horses some oats, one of the guards called to me to run or he would shoot, As I was on a log covered with ice and near the middle of the stream, this was not an easy task, however I turned and went back but did not fall in the river as he had expected I would do. I admit I was a little nervous. After going back they sent one of the men with me, but he would not cross, so remained until I came back with the horses and told me he would not cross on the log for the whole United States.

That afternoon one of the soldiers that had been left behind his company because he was sick, a small skinny cur, commenced to abuse the Mormons and called them all the blasphemous names he could think of. My patience gave way and I drew my arm back and knocked him down when he slipped back into the cook room and told the cook that he had scared that Mormon. The cook, who had seen and heard all that was going on, replied: "I think that Mormon scared you", and when the men came into supper, the cook told them how things stood and from that time on I was a jolly good fellow with them all. We played all kinds of games, running, jumping, wrestling, and had all sorts of fun, and I could hold my own with the best of them, being a pretty good athlete myself.

After staying there four days the rest of the men returned and the Captain told me I could go, and to travel that day until I caught up to the last emigrant train, and to stay with them until we got to Salt Lake, and if I did not I would be arrested and kept a prisoner all winter.

He gave me provisions enough to last me three or four days, as the men at the camp had stolen everything I had that was loose. I started out about noon to make forty miles that day, but I had only gone five miles when my best horse gave out and I could not go any faster than a walk, so I had to tie him back and pull the wagon with one horse. I got to the emigrants about two o'clock in the morning, with one of the horses almost given out. Next morning, I borrowed a mule from a doctor who had been traveling with the emigrant train for a few days. Finally, the doctor went ahead and my sick horse not being able to go as fast as he did, I remained with the company and at last had to leave my sick horse and wagon near Park City and came to the city on my well horse.

After coming home I joined the second company of artillery of the Nauvoo Legion, under Captain Edward Martin. Soon afterwards I was detailed to guard the county court house, as a man named Jason Luce was there condemned to death for killing a man named Sam Bunting, which took place on Main Street at the Salt Lake Hotel. I stayed at the court house at night for six weeks until he was shot. After this I worked for the Church for a while driving team and then took a trip south with Bryant Stringham to find good herding grounds for the church cattle.

In the fall of 1864 I took a trip to the Muddy Country, about one hundred miles south of St. George. William Harrison, William Davis and myself left Salt Lake about the first of December with one wagon, two mules and horses, and necessary tools for making a home and farm.

We took flour and provisions enough to last us a year. It snowed nearly every day but we traveled until we go to Wild Cat Canyon, where we found the snow had drifted from three to eight feet deep and it took us three days to go about a mile, having to dig our road through the snow. We dug a hole in the snow, made a fire in the middle, making beds on one side of the fire so as to keep from freezing. In the day time we could keep ourselves warm shoveling snow, but the glare of the sun on the snow made us snow-blind. I was the last one to get blind, but it lasted much longer than the others, however we were all pretty sick.

We got to Beaver City at last and rested up. The winter was a very cold one, and we could not buy enough hay for our horses so when we came to a quaking aspen grove we would cut down the trees and our horses would eat the bark off the limbs. After we got to the Black Ridge, about forty miles north of St. George, there was plenty of good feed for our teams, and hay was six cents per pound. We paid three dollars for an arm full of corn, flour and other things in proportion. Our stay in St. George was short, and continued our travel south soon, passing the last settlement, we were in the most desolate country imaginable. The Virgin River is a pretty large stream so full of mud and sand and poison springs that we were all sick. We were three o stream so full of mud and sand and poison springs that we were all sick. We were three of the first settlers out of fifteen who settled on the Muddy, with Captain Smith as our acting Bishop and he was indeed a fine man. In mid-winter the Muddy Country will produce anything that you can grow in the north in the summer time. I saw wheat almost ripe and three feet high. I took up some land, cleared off the brush and thought I would make my home there. I was appointed, together with another man, and an Indian guide, to prospect the country and see what resources there were for lumber to build houses with. We found plenty about sixty miles distant, but a poor chance to make a road as the country is composed of sand and rock and very little vegetation.

We found the ancient ruins of a race of people that are now extinct, some large buildings almost covered the top over with sand, and also the homes of the ancient cliff dwellers. We stayed there all winter and in the spring left all our things in charge of Captain Smith and came back to Salt Lake City. I took a trip to Cache Valley and like the north country so much better than the south that I concluded not to go back to the Muddy.

A few incidents about the trip to the Southern Utah: After leaving St. George there are a few settlements on the Santa Clara river, the last one being Jacob Hamlin's. He was the Indian interpreter in that country at the time, 1865, as he was married to some of the Indian Squaws and lived on the outskirts of civilization. In passing his place we had a talk with him about our journey. He advised us to keep on the River Virgin as near as possible, and follow the river until we got to the Muddy River.

He told us that when we made our camp at night that two Indians were sure to camp with us that night, no matter whether we had seen an Indian that day or not. He told us that they would take extra care of our horses and bring them to camp the next morning, and all they would want was a camp kettle of mush, so on our camping that night we looked for some Indians to herd our horses, but there was none in sight. No sooner had our camp been made and our fire lighted than two Indians appeared from whence we did not now. We asked them to "pooney wooney" (herd our horses) and they consented, so we prepared a kettle of boiling mush and placed it before them. They sat on the other side of the kettle and stuck two fingers into the pot of hot much and kept a stream of mush going from the pot to their mouth until the kettle was empty, after which they scraped a hole in the sand and were going to lie down and go to sleep. We told them to take our horses out to feed and they told us they would in the morning. When the sun went down all our persuasive powers did not move them, for they would not work when their stomachs were full, so we let them lay there and we drove our horses across the river. The next morning they brought them back to camp and wanted more mush. They had fooled us once and from then on we made them do their work before they got their pay. At every camp we made, the Indians would show up, not the same ones, but one or two different ones, and we would feed them in the morning.

The country south of St. George is practically bare of vegetation; sand bed full of prickly pears and a few tall trees with a bunch of leaves on top. The trunks of the trees are covered with dead leaves and they are called the Joshua tree. There is also a giant cactus, it grows from four to eight feet high and is from one to two feet in diameter. It is round like a spot and has thorns all over it, about four inches long, and is full of water of a disagreeable taste and smell. They are said to have saved people on the desert from perishing. It is strange but everything in the vegetable line has a thorn on it.

The Piute Indians are of a smaller type than the rest of the tribes I have seen, very few of them standing more than five feet high, but they are extremely well built, resembling the Japanese. At the time I was there they wore no clothes except a band made by the squaws, which they wore around their loins and they were considered the lowest type of Indian in America. They had no horses or guns, their only means of defense being their bows and arrows, with which they were experts. They would watch for hours to shoot a lizard, the body of which would weigh about half a pound. I once took part in an Indian wedding. There were two young bucks who wanted the same girl, and to decide the question they chose up sides of about ten in number, and each young man-made camp about half a mile apart and the girl was placed half way between. The buck that was successful in getting the girl to the goal first was the lucky man. They would push and pull the girl from side to side, being permitted to hit with their hands and throw each other down, but could use nothing but their hands and feet. There were three white men in the fight, two on the side of the buck that the girl wanted and one on the other side. I tell you it was a great time we had, knocking the bucks down and pulling them back and helping the girl to the goal she wanted to gain. When the girl was going in the direction she did not want to go, she would pull back and lie down and catch hold of the brush and fight and do the best she could to go the other way, but as soon as she would get in the direction she wanted to go she would run and laugh defiance at the enemy. At last we won, being on the side the girl wanted to win, and we got her to the goal and the ceremony was performed, though the disappointed one did not appear to take his defeat very hard.

After seeing Cache Valley, where all my folks lived, I concluded to make my home there, so I bought a small farm and a city lot, built a log house and after one year concluded to get married and settle in Logan.

I arranged my affairs so that when I got married we would move up to Logan and commence life as farmers, but that was not to be, for when I was married to Mary Catherine Bullock she would have to leave her widowed mother all alone and as she was growing old and did not have good health we concluded to stay with her for a while, which I never regretted. My wife was four years younger than I was, being born the 4th February, 1847 and I was born on the 4th February 1843. We did not have any trouble to keep our birthdays as they were on the same day of the same month. A few days after our marriage in the endowment house on the Temple Block, I went to work for the Church again, under my old friend Bryant Stringham. My work consisted of a variety of team work, driving cattle to the herd grounds and sometimes assisting on the Mormon Tabernacle, which was the first arched roof built in America or in any other country. There was not an iron pin in it, all the timber being put together with Utah pine dowels or pins and the thousands of holes that had to be bored took many months to do.

Every piece of wood was framed and put together on the ground, then taken apart and put in its proper place in the roof. After forty years it is apparently as sound and good as any roof in the city. Henry Grow was the master mechanic from first to last, and it stands as a monument to his skill and perseverance in those early days. We had no coal to burn so had to get all our fuel from the canyons.

One day, being short of fire wood, I borrowed a yoke of cattle and a wagon from the Tithing Office, and started up Big Cottonwood Canyon for a load of wood. I remember well the date, June 13th, because that was the day of the highest water for many years. About fourteen miles on my journey the water was so in places that it was hard to distinguish the river from the road. At one place my cattle took the shortest cut and tried to cross the river, which of course was an impossibility. I could have saved myself from getting in the river, but having a goodly supply of bedding which I tried to save and in doing so got so far into the river that I could not get to shore. I made a jump toward the shore but in a second my wagon, cattle, and myself were swept down the river. Being somewhat of a swimmer and considered one of the best in town, I was not frightened at first, but all my experience in swimming did not help me as I could not get my head out of the water and I went down the stream, sometimes rolling and other times headlong, and in every possible way except the right way, until I gave up all hopes of seeing my wife and child again. During my stay in the water my whole life passed before me like a panorama, from my earliest recollections up to that time and I did not fear for myself as I felt that I might have done worse and made a complete failure of my salvation, but my thoughts were for my poor wife and child. What would become of them when I did not return? They did not expect me back for three days and I pictured my wife's grief when she found out the worst and in my mind I could see my body covered up with sand and the summer sun beating down upon my corpse, and the horrible sight it would be when it was found. In fact it is not possible for me to describe the thoughts and feelings that passed through my mind. Well, after going about fifty rods under water, I rose to the top and was washed to the side and my right arm caught over a rock and my leg braced another rock under the water, but I was helpless for some time. I could not breather for sometime and I felt as though my senses would leave me. If ever a man sent up a silent prayer to his Maker, I did at that time. There was I, wedged against a rock wall with the current of water crowding me, and yet so near deliverance and could not help myself. After a while I began to breath a little and appeared to gather strength, and it was then that I was afraid of loosing my senses. After trying for sometime to drag myself out of the water, for I was still under the water, it seemed as if some unseen power came to my assistance. I lay on my stomach for some time, for I was not able to rise, and when I tried to stand I reeled like a drunken man, and the river seemed to be trying to draw me back into it. After sometime I began to get my strength back and I walked up the Canyon to see if my cattle had gotten off as well as myself. About twelve rods above where I got out I saw part of my wagon and about ten rods from there I saw one of my oxen straddled on a rock in the river. Near the side the other ox had gotten out of the water and had the yoke on his neck. I went back to the part of the wagon that I had seen and I found the thick rope and binding chain and my ax were still on the wagon, so with great fear and trembling I mustered up courage enough to wade out to the wagon to get the rope, chain and ax, and then went back to the ox that had gotten out. I threw the rope over the head of the ox that had gotten out. I threw the rope over the head of the ox that was still in the water, tied the end of the rope to the other ox, and together we dragged him out. After making an ox bow of a choke-cherry wood, I got my cattle together and what was left of the wagon and started for home. I stayed that night at Cottonwood at my wife's uncles, Alexander Hill, and got home next day. After telling my wife about the accident I took a bath and while I was changing my clothes my wife came in the room, and after looking at me she began to cry for she said that my body was black and blue all over. I knew that I was sore and stiff but did not know I was so badly bruised as I did not feel the bumps that I got in the water.

After resting up a few days I again went to work. My next try was taking a herd of cattle to Fillmore to the Church herd grounds. On my return we came home on the west side of Utah Lake. While stopping for noon on the shore of the lake, it being very hot, some of the boys went in the lake to swim, and I concluded to do likewise. I asked one of the boys if it was deep enough for me to dive, for I made a practice of going into the water head first. He said it was some six feet deep at the edge, so I took a run and dove in, and when my hands struck the bottom I found that I could hold my breath no longer, and with about fifteen feet of water to raise through, and when the top was reached I was exhausted and everything looked red to me. The boys saw that there was something wrong with me and came to my help and got me to shore.

I was so sick and weak that I could not drive the team home and had to be propped up in the wagon. After getting home I was quite sick and in a few days the skin all over my body began to scale and eventually there grew a new outside skin and my health returned.

That fall I worked in the hay field on the Church Farm. Bryant Stringham was in charge, who told me to put up the largest stack of hay that had ever been put up in Utah. When completed it contained about two hundred tons, but it was a failure as it took too much hay to top it out and about one fourth of the hay spoiled by rain and snow. In those days we did not have derricks to life the hay with, but it was all pitched by hand, while the cutting was done with scythes and raked by hand. About ten men in a row would cut the grass and it was a pretty sight to see them all making a stroke at the same time. One man would start to mow and when he had cut about five feet, the next one would start, then the next and so on until all would be cutting at the same time. Every man had the same chance as the last man on the row took the lead on the next row, so that the fast mower did no more than the slow one. It was my privilege to run one of the first Buckeye mowers that came to Utah, which cost about $500.00, which is accounted for by the freight rate of 25¢ per pound from the Missouri River to Utah, having to be hauled by ox teams and taking eighty-five days to make the trip, across the plains.

The next trip south I started on the first of the new year and was gone eight days. I left my family well and enjoying new year's fun, but when I returned my wife's mother was dead and buried. The day she was buried I drove a team of mules one hundred and thirteen miles, from Chicken Creek to Salt Lake City. It was a long drive in one day but the mules were none the worse for it next day.

When my first child was about two months old we moved over to the Church Island, better known as Antelope Island. The lake was rising fast at that time and we crossed the lake on a large flat boat built to carry fifty head of wild horses. We had a fine trip crossing the lake. My work on the Island consisted in building fences, planting orchards, tending garden, breaking wild horses, milking cows, etc. There was another family there at that time, and the work was pleasant and we enjoyed ourselves. We had all the milk, chickens, vegetables, fruit and other necessary eatables and plenty of it. We enjoyed boating and bathing in the lake. The branding of wild horses made some excitement as some of them were very ferocious and would fight. During one of our branding times a man by name of William Ashby was kicked and knocked down and senseless. He had the flesh cut on his forehead and eyebrow so that it fell down his cheek. I cleansed the wound, soaked it in arnica, and sewed it back in place all before he came to his sense. It was a bad cut but when healed it did not show very much. At another time a boy fell from his horse and broke his arm above the elbow. We made some wooden splints, set the bones, bandaged it up and he got well without the aid of a doctor.

We had one horse that was very hard to get into the corral, which would break and run, leading the rest with him every time we got them near the corral, so we decided to catch him and take him off the Island. We started to catch him early in the morning, and ran him until dark, then we started at day-break and kept him on the run all that day. On the third day about 10:00 o'clock, the horse ran on a long point of the land into the lake and we followed him, put a rope on him and took him to the barn. He was naturally a good trotting horse but was never much good afterward as his heart was broken.

In the fall the other family went back to Salt Lake City, and my wife accompanied them. A young lady, Louise Ashby and myself, were left on the Island alone, with the understanding that the boat would return in about three days. The days came and went and no boat arrived. Three weeks had passed and no boat, so we began to think something serious had happened. I looked to see if there was anything we could cross the lake on, but could find nothing suitable, as they had taken all three boats with them, and it was seven miles to shore. We put in our times as best we could, Miss Ashby cooking and making butter and I would milk the cows, being

35

forty-two to be milked night and morning there was plenty to occupy the time. When the third week had passed, Miss Ashby took sick and could not eat or sleep. Day after day she lingered and grew very feverish. I did not know what to do for her and it looked as though she would die and what was I to do with her body. The thought almost drove me mad as I was nervous about my wife who had gone to the city to have an operation performed. I could not sleep at night for the thought of conditions and wondering why they did not come for us, and the young lady getting weaker every day. My time was taken up during this time as I had everything to do and watch over the sick girl.

After four weeks had gone the girl got some better and would take a little nourishment and was able to get out on the porch. Just three days later we saw Bryant Stringham, with another family and a lot of boys coming toward the Island in the boat. The reason they were so long returning was because the Indians had run off with some of the Church cattle down south, and Stringham had taken all the boys he could find and gone after them, which took longer than he had expected it would. I was glad to see my wife who was looking much better and had got well, so I felt paid for my anxiety.

The lonesomeness of an Island with someone sick night unto death is too terrible to describe, especially when there is no means of escape. My nerves were so unstrung that I could not sleep and one night I had an idea that the place was haunted. About midnight I heard a noise and, at first, I thought it was mice, so I got up and tried to drive them away, but when I moved to another part of the room the noise seemed to follow me. No matter what part of the room I was in the noise was there, and I began to think it was a bad omen and yet I did not believe in spooks or ghosts. At last the noise stopped and I fell asleep but the next night at about the same time it started again and I confess I was scared to stay in the house, so I took my blankets and went out to the hay stack for the rest of the night. Early the next morning I went to the girl's room to see how she was feeling and noticed she was tapping on the wall and scraping the adobes with her fingers. I went to my room and discovered that it was the same noise I had heard in the night and was ashamed of myself for being so superstitious.

Sometime after this I was sent down south to take charge of a band of cattle on a new ranch on the Sevier River. There were a number of boys at first but as we got the ranch in shape some of them returned to the city. The following were left on the ranch; William Davis, Frank Hume, James Darton, Al Tanner and myself. We got our camps located and our cattle accustomed to the place and about three months later I concluded to go to the city to make a report, and especially to see my wife and child. It was about thirty-five miles to the nearest town by the road. There were Indian trails on the other side of the river which cut the trip down to eighteen miles to the settlement, so I concluded to take the trail. J. Darton wanted to go along as his father lived in the settlement, and William Davis said he would go, so as to accompany Darton back to the ranch. We started out, found the trail and got to Nephi early in the evening.

We put up at the house of the Bishop who made us

welcome and asked us which way we came, to which we replied; "By the Indian Trail". He looked surprised and asked us if we saw any Indians. We answered no, and then he told us that the Black Hawks had broken out and were killing the whites and stealing the horses and cattle. The very day we came they had brought one man who was killed on the trail we had followed.

Two men were returning from a ranch and the Indians were concealed in some rocks in the worst place along the trail. They had killed one man and filled the other with arrows, but he escaped and reached Nephi with seven arrows in his body. One had to be pushed through his body as it could not be pulled out of his back.

We felt queer when we heard of these things having happened, but I told the boys we must go back to the ranch next morning, but they refused to go, saying they would not risk their lives for all the cattle on the ranch, and I was a fool to risk mine. I tried to show them that it was cowardly to allow me to go alone, but as there were still two boys on the ranch that did not know the Indians were bad, I thought we ought to go. I told the Bishop I would start back at day-break and he tried to persuade me not to go and said if I would wait until Sunday (this being Friday) that he would call a meeting and get a dozen men to go back with me. I said it was too long to wait, so at the first sign of day I got up, gave my horses a good grooming and small feed of oats, called the other boys but they refused to get up, so I started for the trail. I had gone about seven miles when I noticed some fresh tracks going the same direction I was. I thought it was early for white men to be on the trail and I saw that the horse did not have shoes on so concluded that it was Indians. In a short time I was convinced that it was Indians and that they were not far ahead of me, and I began to feel very uneasy. I had to follow the trail for about three miles that was rocky and very hard for a horse to travel faster than three miles an hour. There was a deep gully on one side and a high mountain on the other, and if the Indians got there first they could hide and get me at the same point they got other men the night before. I still followed them and concluded to take my chances of getting to the ranch. After traveling about twelve miles I saw some smoke and concluded they had made camp and were getting ready for me to pass them.

Their camp was at the mouth of a narrow pass and there were plenty of rocks they could hide behind and my chances were slim of getting passed them. I thought of turning back while there was a chance to escape, but my pride would not let me do that. I thought of the two boys at the camp who did not know that the Indians were bad and how would it look for me to turn back and not warn them of the danger they were in. I concluded I would not go back as I had started out against the advice of the people of the settlement and I would see it through, come what would. I thought it was bad enough to be a coward but worse to let the people see how cowardly I was and decided to go on my way.

I saw their horses, twelve of them, picketed out to feed, but there was not an Indian in sight. I looked to see if there were any among the rocks, but there was not a sign of an Indian, so all fear left me and I road up to the campfire and gave an Indian Hoop, all the while looking up at the rocks. All at once twelve guns were fired over my head and as many white men stood around me and commenced asking me questions and calling me a fool to follow their trail for they had purposely traveled as Indians to lead me on, for they first saw me they thought I was an Indian and thought to trap me. When they saw me coming toward them and saw that I was a white man, they decided to scare me and took that means of doing it. They asked me the reason I was out on that Indian trail alone and I told them. They told me they were a posse sent to guard another crowd of men at the cattle ranch twelve miles down the river. When they found that I was going to their camp they covered themselves with their saddle blankets so that they could not be see and when I was looking up at the rocks they jumped up and fired their guns.

After a little talk they decided to accompany me to our camp and find out if I had told them the truth. They did not think I was such a fool as they first took me to be and told my two companions that they could feel safe as long as they had such a captain. They told the boys how they had shot over my head and apparently did not scare me much really made more of the affair than was necessary. They soon left the camp and after telling the boys the conditions of the Indians and about the two men killed so near our camp, we commenced to make a place of safety in case we were surprised by the red men. Our camp stood about five rods back from the river bank which was about six feet above the water. We commenced digging the hole about ten feet square near the level of the water and on the side next to the river we dug a hole below the surface of the water so we could get light and water. We next dug a tunnel from the hole to our camp and brought the opening under our tent. We covered the hole with poles and willows and finished it up with dust and then three all our firewood on top of that. Soon we had a good stock of provisions cooked and put in the dugout. Our intentions were that if the Indians made a raid on us we would jump down the tunnel and crawl through to our dug out and there could stand them off for sometime and they could not starve us out, as we could stay a long time on bread and water.

It would not be safe for them to crawl through the tunnel as we could settle with them as only one could come at a time, and they would be at a great disadvantage. However, we were not troubled with them. Once or twice we thought there was trouble and got ready to hide, but they were false alarms. I had a pretty scare once, however. It was our rule to keep the cattle out of the bend of the river close by, but we kept one riding horse in the bend so we could get our horses quick. We likewise kept one saddle horse ready for use at the camp, tied up night and day. One morning as I was cooking breakfast, my attention was attracted by a noise in the willows in our horse bend, and I jumped on the horse and went down to see what was the trouble. When I got there I saw that someone was driving the cattle and of course I concluded that it was an Indian. I got behind and traveled as fast as my horse could go and very soon my suspicions proved to be true, for about twenty rods in front of me was an Indian in a buffalo robe, driving the cattle. I looked about me to see if there was any more of them and concluded he was alone, so I thought I would make a good Indian of him. I braced my nerves, took aim and just as I was to shoot my horse turned side ways and I did not shoot. I got a little closer and took aim and was about to pull the trigger when a bunch of willows came between us. At last I got within twenty feet of him on a straight trail and held my pistol on the spot and was about to pull the trigger when the man let out a yell to the cattle and I recognized the voice. It was one of the boys who had seen the cattle in the bend and gathered up the buffalo robe and had gone to drive them out, instead of using a horse for that purpose. To say that I was scared is putting it lightly. I shook from head to foot and a deathly feeling came over me so that I could not ride the horse but had to walk to camp. When I scolded him and told him how near he came to being shot, he laughed at me and asked me if I was sorry I had not shot him. I admitted I had talked to him rather hard.

About six weeks later, Bryant Stringham brought twenty cow boys and gathered up the cattle and we broke camp. At the time of these exciting experiences they are not as harassing to the feelings as one would think, but looking back I realize the danger more than I did at the time they happened.

In 1870 there was a call for volunteers to settle Soda Springs, Idaho, so I concluded to go there. I got two yoke of cattle, one cow, and a good wagon that had been fitted up for a sheep-herder, secured a Government tent, good supply of provisions, and started out. After a hard trip, I arrived at Soda Springs and found that all the desirable land was claimed by Delegate William Hooper and Company, and lots were $200.00 each. Through my helping to survey the townsite I got one lot for $125.00, built a two roomed log house and a barn, fenced the lot and moved my family there in the spring. I planted a nice garden with all kinds of vegetables the same as they had in Salt Lake City. The land is very productive in that part and the garden was as fine a one as there was in that part of the country.

On the 3rd of July, Captain Hooper stopped at my place and looked over the garden and told me it was all a mistake to say that farming could not be done there as he had never seen better gardens in Utah; potatoes in blossom, corn two feet high and other things in proportion.

I was certainly proud of my garden, but on the 3rd of July, 1871, the frost nipped all the vegetation and on the morning of the 4th, when the sun came up, everything turned black and all my labors were lost so far as my garden was concerned. Still, I had not reason to complain as there was plenty of work with good pay. I did some fencing and took contracts to build log houses like the one I had for myself. I did considerable trading in cattle and horses, Soda Springs being the last trading post for about one hundred miles. The men that were driving cattle from Texas to Oregon were glad to trade their lame cattle for those that could travel. At times I would get two or three for one and often paid cash. During the time I was there I got together a nice little herd of cattle and horses. The first winter was very cold and the snow was about four feet deep, and lasted about five months, but we had plenty of hay put up for the stock and did not want for anything ourselves. When spring came the snow left in a hurry and did not leave the street muddy as it sank into the earth.

I took a contract to do some fencing and was doing well financially and I had several men working for me and prospects were bright indeed.

My wife was about to become a mother again and it was hard to get a doctor and midwives were scarce, but at last I got an old lady who had brought many children into the world and our first son was born on the 12th of July. My wife did not get along as well as she should have done, so the midwife gave her a sweat and put cold clothes on her which brought on congestion and chills which turned to convulsions, eight or ten times in one day. I thought she was dying, and it resulted in paralysis.

We got a doctor from Fort Hall and he gave me some hopes of her getting better as she was a young woman and healthy prior to this, but he told me that it was likely to come back in seven years, which proved too true.

There I was with two children and my wife lying as if dead, and only a foster brother, J. L. Farnes, a small boy, to care for them, so I sent to Bear Lake and got and old lady and her two nieces to help me. I did not need them all but could not get one without the others, and none of them could change a baby, so I had to do that myself. One woman fifty, with a large family, one twenty-five, married, and one eighteen and none of them able to wash a new born baby. How does that look for women who hire out as nurses? My wife continued in the same state for about a month, when she improved so she could move some of her limbs, and in three months we moved to Logan where most of our folks lived, and there she got the attention she needed and began to improve rapidly, but our baby died when about three months old. O! The night he died I shall never forget. It was a terrible stormy night; the wind blew and the rain came down in torrents. There I lay by the side of my wife with the baby in my arms trying to keep him warm as we knew he was very sick. At last over come by constant watching, I fell asleep, and when I awoke, found that the baby had died on my arm while I, its father, was asleep, and its mother too sick to do anything for it. I cannot describe my feelings at the time. I got up and called my sister, Matilda, and got her to take the baby in the other room, and then woke my wife. As soon as she woke she missed the baby and I told her it was in the other room, that it was very sick and perhaps it would die. She answered "It is dead or it would not be in the other room". I told her it was dead and she said she knew it was as soon as she missed it from the bed. After the funeral the place seemed so quite and still that my nerves gave out and there did not seem much for me to do, as I had had sole charge of the baby for nearly three months, and now it was all over. In a few weeks my wife began to get better, except that she would take horrible convulsions at times. Sometimes she would take six convulsions in a day and this kept up for two years. During this time we always kept a horse saddled and bridled and a boy ready to come and fetch me home, for all the time I expected her to die in one of those fits. About this time the fits left her and she became strong and was able to do her house work. During the next five years she bore two more girls, Emily and Edith.

The two oldest girls, Annie and Elizabeth, were born

before we went to Soda Springs. In 1878, in September, I married my second wife, Josephine Fjelstead and in October, 1879, she bore me a son, Willard H. Farnes. Both my wives lived in the same house in separate apartments, and Josephine was a great help to my first wife.

During the seven years after my wife's sickness I had sold my place in Soda Springs and was running a butcher shop in Logan, and was doing well financially, but at the end of seven years the worst sorrow came to me when my wife Mary, died. The day she died she got up as usual and we got breakfast and I was about to go to my work. She asked me if it was necessary for me to go to the shop that day, and stated that she would like me to stay home. I told her I would remain if it was her wish. About 10:00 o'clock in the morning she said she was not feeling very well, so I told her to go and lie down for a while. She replied that if she went to bed she would never get up again. I told her not to talk that way, for she would live for a long time yet. She replied that she knew she would not, and so did I. I was afraid she spoke too true, as the doctor from Fort Hall that first visited her said she might get over it, but it was likely to return in seven years, and if it did, she would die.

I do not know how she knew that her sickness might return in seven years, for I had not told a living soul that would tell her what the doctor had said about it returning. While we were talking together, I noticed that her face began twitching and soon she had one of those fits and a horrible convulsion, and she never spoke again, for she had a convulsion every twenty minutes until 10:00 o'clock at night, and died at that time. There was I, left with four little motherless children, and to try to express my sorrow and grief at that time is beyond my power.

We laid her beside her baby boy, our first-born son, on the hill, and prayed God that I might live so that I would meet her again in the spirit world and embrace her again.

Josephine took care of Mary's children and raised them to womanhood, and proved as good a step mother to them as was possible for a woman to be. Josephine, my second wife, has had nine children, three girls and six boys. Two boys died when about eighteen months old, George died with membrane croup and Melville died with diphtheria. I have had born to me fourteen children, five by my first wife, Mary Catherine Bullock, and nine to my wife Josephine Fjeldsted. At the present writing we have eight children married; Mary Ann to C. C. Cressall of Logan, Edith to George H. Budd, Willard H. to Barbara Brown, Frances Josephine to Alfred A. Thomas of Richmond, Utah, Clarence LeRoy to Mary Hagen, California, Alice Laverne to Park Kenner of Salt Lake. The children unmarried are, Veta Catherine, nineteen years old, Frank Donald, sixteen years, and Rodney Bryant, twelve years old. My wife, Veta Josephine, was fifty-two years old August 5th 1909, and I was sixty-seven years old, February 4th, 1910.

INDEX